hold the note

hold the note

Domenico Capilongo

QUATTRO BOOKS

The publication of *hold the note* has been generously supported by the Canada Council for the Arts and the Ontario Arts Council.

 Canada Council for the Arts · Conseil des Arts du Canada   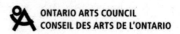 ONTARIO ARTS COUNCIL CONSEIL DES ARTS DE L'ONTARIO

Cover painting: Lise Fournier
Author's photograph: Rob Ackerman, robackerman.com
Cover design: Diane Mascherin
Typography: Grey Wolf Typography

Library and Archives Canada Cataloguing in Publication

Capilongo, Domenico
    Hold the note / Domenico Capilongo.

Poems.
ISBN 978-1-926802-08-4

    1. Jazz--Poetry. 2. Italian Canadians--Poetry. 3. Family--Poetry. I. Title.

PS8605.A64H64 2010   C811'.6   C2010-905322-2

Poetry Series #14
Published by Quattro Books Inc.
89 Pinewood Avenue
Toronto, Ontario, M6C 2V2
www.quattrobooks.ca

Printed in Canada

for Cole and Emil

Contents

after nine

jazzista

the alchemy of brass

the air. the breath pushed through the lungs of thought.
past the heart beating a metronome of flesh. out the
mouth mad with the echoes of lost sounds. merging past
the embouchure of lips into tubes of brass. spirals split
atoms. modify the internal makeup of meaning. melt into
the brass alloy of time. willing the transformation of
dreams from one dimension to the next and back again.
out the horn's bell. puffing up the night. a scared fog
seeping into the crevice of your ear. tickling the back of
your brain. down the spinal column of memory to the
base of everything. heating the tissue of this moment.
still warm from breath to deepest touch.

the true eventual story of buddy bolden

"His mind became the street." – Michael Ondaatje

man could play the horn in syncopated loud clear liquid
notes. seeping, pouring into the corners of the mid-
afternoon streets of storyville. people would stop fucking
just to let the sound wash over them. a blue rain of
heartbeats.

buddy heard voices in his head. heard notes. heard
armstrong. heard dizzy and miles in his bones. heard
them deep in the cranium of time. before it folds into the
saturated future. the jasmine scent of everything to come.
heard his mind march into the endless night like a sweet
lie until the air fell apart.

*in the parade sun beating down. I could hear the street under
my shoes. I heard her voice. what she said to me and I blew
my horn. I blew louder than a man would dare. I heard and
I listened and that's when I inhaled. I pulled the world in
through that horn. I sucked up colour. sucked up the memory
of long summer grass. pulled it in. the note played through my
body came out my toes the top of my head. I felt it in the pits
of my eyes. I sucked that horn whole and followed the sound
away.*

savoy ballroom

dizzy on the bandstand
like a blow fish
his head about to burst open
the be-bop pops
the night into a string of stars
jitterbug contest about to start
he jumps down
takes the hand of the girl beside me
goes and wins the thing
just like that

so what?

the way he enters the song is the way you want to enter a
room. like that cool breeze through a post-coital
bedroom window. hold yourself upright easy not tense.
walking not too fast but not too slowly either. the turn-
your-head-to-look-at-him disruption. the I-don't-give-
a-fuck way your hips move. soft fumble of your legs. feet
pour across the floor. you're late but you're not gonna
show it matters. you're never late 'cuz the shit can't start
till you get there. when it does. man look out. one note is
gonna fill this room.

my favourite things
while listening to John Coltrane

these are them
my faves in rows
in coloured bows
I like them in between toes
listening to the flow
of these things held
dear in fires
in smoke
I'd grab them in tow
'cuz these things are my favourite
blowing through afternoons
through tunes
feel the weight of last night's date
have you made your list?
have you dusted them off?
keep them safe and light
don't let anyone finger them
these are mine
I'll show you one day
and you'll say
so these are them?
I'll answer in twisted syllables
turn the lights off in pirouettes
throw away the key
and try and find
where you're hiding
'cuz these are my
favourite things
before sundays
before wine
and the wilderness of kisses

billie @ 120 km

through open fingers
out the window
whistling ring-finger
dying afternoon

the echoing passenger seat
close my eyes
through the clarinet solo
just for a second
           just for a second

everyone's doing it
after Cole Porter

in condominium corners
romantic sponges
parked cars
clams against their will
in crowded shopping malls
lazy jellyfish
between sheets
in shallow shores
under folds
in the privacy of bowls
on mountain tops
goldfish do it
on the radio
sentimental centipedes
on cell phones
courageous kangaroos
beneath the moon
giraffes on the sly
in the middle of the street
sweet guinea pigs
on the kitchen countertop
bears in pits
at the back of poetry readings
let's

armstrong in the coliseum

raises his trumpet. sends out a honey-dipped sleepy time
like the emperor just gave him the thumbs-down. feels
the hot breath of the sword against his neck. the slice of
the lion's roar. he stands blood ankle deep. pushes his
voice up to the peasant cheap seats.

sittin' on the stones of rome.

makes me wanna say I'm home.

people everywhere stop and sit and stare.

make my trumpet want to blare . . .

loves spaghetti. loves the way italian mineral water
bubbles up his insides. the sound of his trumpet. his
voice bounces echoes through imperial streets up spanish
steps. the night filling with the taste of it.

voice

"I try my best to chug, stomp, weep, whisper, moan, wheeze, scat, blurt, rage, whine and seduce." – *Tom Waits*

the rumble of a stomach
from the pit of this thought
guttural whispers in the mind's throat
a broken blender full of bones
stones ground down for hard-cocked potions
deep moan of frogs over forgotten graves
death rattle of leather crickets
the sound of the moon reflecting
off shards of cheap wine bottles
in the inner ear the echo
       in the inner ear the
in the inner ear
       in the inner
in the
       in

walks into the speakeasy

like he's the bee's knees and we're all wet but I can tell
he's already splifficated neck deep in giggle water drunk
probably at home made by his cousin some turpentine
moonshine.

the flappers take another drag of their long cigarettes
and pretend not to notice. it's the way he leans up to the
bar that hushes the room. the band kicks it up a notch.
couples spice up the dance floor with saucy charleston
side steps. in whispers at tables everyone thinks but
doesn't ask and wonders when or if he'll take the stage
fill the night with his smooth sweet breath.

monk

and they ask him. stop him on his way to the piano
mumbling to himself. I didn't believe it till I saw it. the
mumbling. "thelonious," they say, "mr. monk you often
wear different hats when you play." and you can see it. his
eyes acknowledging the camera like it was some alien.
see the way he sort of fidgets? he'd rather be at the piano.
his body turned off to the side too big for the bench. feet
moving uncomfortable in his own skin. "do you think the
hats have an effect on the music?" you can hear the pause
between notes. his brain composing an off-beat melody
minutes before twelve. he mumbles something and then
you can almost hear him say, "what the fuck, man? it's
just a fucking hat. listen to me play. listen to the damn
music. let it fill you up." he shrugs his shoulders like he's
trying to let his jacket fall. says something like, "I don't
know, maybe." his breath trailing, contemplating the
nuance of every note of the question. watch it. listen. see
for yourself.

thelonious monk in a chinese hat

he's playing the piano at breakneck speed. takes one
hand off. fishes through his pocket. pulls out a white
handkerchief. wipes his wet forehead as though he's
drunk. the melody sweating out of him. he punches the
handkerchief down with a clang of notes falling in place
like orange leaves on an autumn picnic basket. both
hands now waltz through 'round midnight in a modal
puff of smoke. removes the cigarette from his mouth
with a flip of his wrist. a *jazzista* magician. places it at
the end of the piano balanced on ivory for later. his
fingers slam chop sloppy french kisses up into the air. all
the while his right foot tapping keeps spastic epileptic
time to the music in his head. he decides to stand up and
dance around the stage like a drunk uncle at a wedding
reception who stumbles into the wrong banquet hall on
his way back from the washroom and lets his body loose
upon the crowd.

hard to be a hep cat

when everyone's down with this or that. hard to keep it
real when they bling the bling and fat the phat. when the
hop is hip and it's pimp to ratatatat and cap some cat
with your gat while you tap bitches and make sure
snitches get stitches for being a rat. I think it's hard to be
a hep daddy-o till my son says *hatpatat* for the cat in the
hat and I'm so down with that 'cuz that's where it's really
at. that's where it's really at. time to swing with the little
cats. *hatpatat*. it's time to swing with the little cats.

mack

and mack's back
      traded in his knife for a tech-nine
      for a hot gat
old mack's back in town
      now he's hardcore

he shot that shark babe
      for his pearly whites
and yeah there's still cement
      in that tugboat for weight

now that mack's back
      look out
'cuz the game's changed
      he sells it homegrown

mack's back
      'cuz you need him
he's on his hands free
      got himself a homepage

mack's back
      in town

how to scat

"Scat doesn't mean anything but just something to give a song a flavor." – Jelly Roll Morton

i.
forget language
        forget syllables of meaning
sounds strung together in the hieroglyphs of words

ii.
become the horn
transform into trombone
melt into a clarinet
suck the saxophone
sex the piano forte

iii.
get a big pot
fill ¾ with water
sink a trumpet or coronet slowly into it
boil for ten minutes
or until it stops its bubble of blues riffs
remove trumpet
pour into a bowl
slurp loudly while standing
serves one

iv.
dooby do
scit scat
bibbity bat bat
sha ba

how jazz can improve your life

let it play
till there's nothing else
till the day leaks out the window
there's nothing but that swing
that improvised syncopation

listen to it till you hear it
listen till you hear
your heart breathing
skin opening to the night

there are no players
no instruments
just the smoke of notes
filling up your body

listen to it
till you hear it
then listen again
then listen
again

cool

walk like jazz
in the afternoon
slip through blades of grass
eating an orange
peeling it slowly
with a flick of the wrist
fill the day with citrus

breathe like jazz
in slow syncopated exhalations
the riffed rhythm of punctuated air
hangs heavy telling the world
that you have something important to say
step up to the microphone
into the spotlight
choose your words without thinking
say whatever pops into your head
your heart
scat out a eulogy
an epitaph
an oxymoronic oration

smile like jazz
start slowly at the edge of your mouth
make them believe it could go either way
then as if you just thought of it
show them your teeth
make them believe
you could give a shit what they think
like a man in a new suit
who has places to go

blow

I will blow this horn of syllables. string the similes in
rising arpeggios. till I make the room full with pregnant
vowel sounds. to sweep up the cobwebbed edges of this
ceiling. blow this horn of internal rhyming sunbursts. of
adjectives describing old lovers finding each other's
bodies as if for the first time. this horn of words becomes
an umbrella of metaphors to mirror the overflow of lost
whispers. I will blow this horn with my last breath of
broken commas. hoping for the moon to split the night.

jazz and the art of the empty hand

my fist is a trumpet as we improv through this kumite. I
kick out a bass drum line towards your head as you come
at me in a flurry of staccato punches. I can feel the
change of tempo the tinkle of piano sidekicks at my
stomach and move in a trombone slide side step catch
the back of your heel as you land I pull your leg out in a
saxophone sweep low down and swinging.

nessun dorma

lullaby

for cole

"...*sing me a lullaby. Sing me the alphabet. Sing me a story I
haven't heard yet.*" – *The Weakerthans*

sing me your day
moments spent
away from me
colours caught in nets

the universe of new words
exhalations of playgrounds
classrooms full up with
the vocabulaire of language

sing me an afternoon of hugs
wrestling I struggle to trap
the growth of your body
soon you will slip my grip easily

sing me a scat-filled lullaby of kisses
let me tell you stories of nonsense
before you fall into sleep

sing me a song
that I can hold onto
as you out-grow me

sing
        me a song
that
        I can
                hold onto
as you out
        grow me

emil

popping peek-a-boo faces
till you're empty with laughter
this hiccup bounce of emotion
can melt away any foul smelling mood indigo

you have disarmed rooms
made grocery store line-ups crumble
with your twinkled-eye stare down
you say:

> *I will look into you*
> *until you stop and see me*
> *see yourself in me*
> *I crack a smile and touch you*
> *until you're warm again*

you are a reincarnation
the next lama
next mahatma
the next groucho marx

I will take you into war zones
sit you down wobbling
at peace negotiation tables
let opposing sides hear the magic of your eyes
let your laughter fill the ears of broken men

crying out from dreams

folds of night flipping
falling teething
in the half-grip
of the crescent moon

you cry out
your voice cracking down
through the monitor
into the cave of this basement
the rhythm of your breathing changes
when you're being chased

run
       jump
fall

       I will catch you
fish you out in hugs
till it's safe again
the night smooth
and stationary

autumn leaves
after Miles Davis

leaves falling all over the room
emil struggles
lisping through the words

                                     trees
                          leaves

hugs me
through sound
space
the fog of the trumpet lifting us
in the in-between of branches

                                   browns
                        oranges

his warm body against my chest
I could step onto the notes
let go of the thickness of air
holding on to your small limbs

                                 up out
                        into
                             clouds

clipping nails

in the *chiaroscuro* of bedtime
clipping nails in the translucent twilight
of the washroom
everything seems to make sense

try not to get too much nail
liable to trap
the sliver of skin
that lets all hell break loose

back straight
deep breaths
the ancient art of clipping
nails passed down for generations
tell a story about bears
to distract

everything makes sense
dead finger nails
fall like sheet music
on a windy day

ten count

for emil

"one, two, three, four...." – Feist

one more kiss before you kick down from me running
bursting into the day. two more hugs on your way to
challenging playground five-year-olds like a fearless
boxer. three sips of water before you yell again at your
brother in an unending cacophony of notes bending the
room into a drunken opera. four more minutes before
you jump on me laughing gripping my neck with all the
little muscles of your body daring me to escape.

one memory

I stop because this could be the one memory he has. the one pre-eight-year-old memory. mine flashing in my mind like 8 mm film. the dog three doors down eating bowls of steaming spaghetti. me in the pre-breakfast hallway walking in my full body pajamas holding my stuffed one-eared doggie. my dad teaching me how to tie my shoes cuddling with my mom while watching the love boat.

I stop because this could be the one memory. me standing over him. he on the couch still in his pajamas. the sound of my voice rattling the windows. neighbourhood watch alarms sounding. asking him for the fifth, sixth, tenth time to get dressed. the clock ticking in my inner ear. I stop.

muskoka pasta

the backseat a rotini of laughter
as we cut through the parmigiano snow
carving deeper into the winter afternoon
the tortellini moon creeping in the rearview

the power's out in the hotel
we stumble through the cannelloni hallway
like overcooked linguine

the four of us cuddle in the ravioli bed
in lasagna layers of pajamas
telling stories of minestrone superheroes
until the gnocchi light bulbs pop back on

goodnight moon
after Margaret Wise Brown

the green room
a cell phone
a red balloon

a digital picture of
a cow jumping over the
international space station
and three bears
sitting on ikea chairs

two little robo-kittens
and a pair of sub-zero mittens
and a little toy eco-house
and a young wireless mouse

and a recycled plastic comb
and an organic brush
and a bowl full of omega 3 mush
and a quiet old lady
doing yoga while whispering hush

good night room
moon
cow jumping
good night energy saving light
and the red balloon
bears
chairs
mittens
and kittens

good night digital clock
bamboo socks
eco-house
mouse

good night
comb
brush
no body
omega 3 mush
and good night to the old lady
doing yoga while whispering hush

good night stars
air
good night unending
noises everywhere

knee

city park. bmx bike with yellow hand grips. summer day
camp games. two boys bullying me. farmer boys just like
the one in class who came to school with a bag of wheat
and said if you chew it long enough it will turn into gum.
I did and it tasted like snot like chewing on old paper.

they taunted me in the park. pushed me and I rolled a
perfect judo shoulder roll like I saw bruce lee do in that
movie. the one in the coliseum in rome. I popped up to
them laughing. I looked down and saw a flap of skin
hanging from my knee. I jumped on my bike and raced
home. my knee stinging and flapping open like a baby
chick's mouth.

the doctor's hands were warm as he injected the needle
to freeze my knee. he turned and brought back scissors.
he cut the flap of skin off in one snip. it had 4 or 5
strands of pubescent leg hair jutting out of it and he
tossed the whole thing into the waste basket.

it's that sound. the thump of my skin. the piece of me
hitting deep into the bass drum of the basket. this echo
of flesh left still in my ears as he sews my leg shut.

horn

when I learned to play the alto sax
all I wanted to do was kiss the girl
playing the french horn
beside me

I wanted to be the french horn
the way she let it sit on her lap
cupping her hand up into it
the spiraling pipes

her pursed lips
licked and pressed against it
I wanted to speak that soft muted french
puffing out from her like taboo smoke

instead I felt the cold belly
of the saxophone between my legs
and the taste of my reed wet and woody

when I say sicily you think mafia

my uncle drove a train in sicily. we woke up early. his son
and I sat up front with him like train robbers. we woke
up before the heat hit. sicily all different and dry out the
speeding window. ten years old. sent for the summer by
myself like a spy for the government. my mother showed
me pictures before leaving pointing out cousins as
though I should somehow know them already. off the
plane I felt like the lost sheep who wandered off now
back again.

the sound of the train balancing through the summer
thick cotton air. wheels cut the jumble of awkward
winter english syllables mixed up in my head like blank
bars of music. the tracks fill slowly with the bleating of
distant sheep. my uncle stops the train at the edge of
some town and we get out to pick prickly *fichi d'india*
carefully off wild bushes. I pull the railroad hat down so
it touches the tips of my ears. I never want to leave this
place. one of the thorns pricks me. I make an oath as the
heat of the train's engine mixes with the afternoon. I will
keep the memory of this place silent like an ancient
village secret.

feathers

the sound of my *nonna*. my mother's mother leaning into
the sink. the shape of her short body hidden in her dress.
the movement of her elbow. the calisthenics recalled
from a long ago sicilian town. from a time of war when
her husband would lend their scale to the butcher for
meat. the sound of rhythmic ripping. thicker than tearing
paper. the crunch of evening snow under my boots on
after dinner walks with my sons brings this moment
back.

my little-boy feet approaching *nonna* at the sink. where
did my father go? did he buy chickens at the grocery
store? she turns. a look as wet as blood in her eye. caught
in the act of some crime of passion. like killing her dead
husband's lover in the corner pew of that forgotten
church. the white of snow-like feathers everywhere.

the constant pump of her plump elbows tearing and
stripping the chicken. its neck limp in the sink like a wet
dishcloth. in half whispered pants. short of breath. she
tells me to go. let her work. protecting me from some
devil that's taken her over. will she dance with the head
around my bed as I sleep? the sound still ringing in my
ears.

tarantella: once bitten

after five courses of food. the uncles are all drunk. the
lights are dimmed and the music starts to play in 6/8
time. transported back. back to sicilian fields where just
rows of rapini away a woman jumps up and screams.
she's been bitten by a spider. townspeople gather with
tambourines. with mandolins. with pots. with pans. the
venom spreading through her body like a slow tender
caress. she starts to dance. stomping her feet. her left arm
raised. her hand hanging over her head like a question
mark. this could go on for days.

it's unlucky to dance the tarantella without a partner.
aunts pull aunts on the dance floor. my nonna in her 80s
pulls younger women. caught in her web to dance with
her. her knees bouncing in staccato rhythms. my nonna
dances the tarantella like a woman on fire. her partner
always tires before she does and sits down. she locks eyes
with me. now I've been bitten.

tarantella: a wedding song

when they played the tarantella the world would turn
upside down
all the adults bouncing and spinning on the dance floor
like drunk spiders at a ladybug picnic

women dancing with women
men sweating like after hours of working in fields
rushing to meet girlfriends behind churches
someone picks up a tambourine
someone plucks a mandolin
they dance for days
if the priest asks
tell him we've been bitten by spiders

      my cousin and I hide under tables
      coming out only to scoop ice cubes
      out of forgotten drinks
      we throw them on the dance floor
      like seeds in ancient fields
      and watch uncles catching wives falling mid-step
      never missing a beat

      we crawl away
      like little spiders
      our screaming mothers
      on the hunt

tarantella: a love dance

the tarantella starts. the room begins to spin. aunts and uncles gravitate to the dance floor. they stomp and pull each other in whirling circles as if they are making summer wine with their feet.

I take your hand. pull you off your seat and kiss your cheek softly like a slow sicilian spider. I pull you onto the dance floor stomping my feet. twirling you with all eyes on us.

you take to this dance as if you were born in taranto or siracusa. as if your nonna taught you when you were a little girl. your skin soaking up the italian sun. your cousin tapping on the tambourine. your uncle strumming an old mandolin.

the movement of your staccato steps warms me. we pull each other through the dance floor our eyes laughing. hearts beating together like spiders weaving secret webs.

seizure

man locks into a seizure like some giant invisible hand
has him in his grip and shakes him around just for the
fuck of it. falls from the staffroom couch hard thud
against the floor as I bite into my veggie samosa. push
the furniture clear. crouch down and watch his body
shake into a new dimension. rub his back watching drool
seep out his mouth. eyes looping back into his head and
then the banging starts. it's a sound you don't forget like
someone kicks a dog. the hollow thump in his lungs. or
the time you pushed your brother down the stairs. the
guy's head is smacking the floor. I wedge my hand
between his skull and the linoleum and wait for the grip
to loosen from his body. if this were the middle ages I
would whisper to the demon. whisper to satan who has
slipped into his soul to dance a dervish *tarantella* up and
down his spine. what would I say? get the fuck out. leave
this man. satan be gone. his body slows its convulsions.
this man. this body. trembling in my palms will never
know how close we were.

christie pits, august 16th 1933

was a swell night till we heard the bats hit. jews gettin' it
hard in the park when the game was over. don't even
remember who won. just remember that summer every
once in a while you'd see some kid wearing a swastika on
his jacket all 'cause this guy named hitler was made the
new head honcho in germany. I wasn't there when it all
went down but I heard they hung some flag or
somethin'. the jews startin' to mix it up. tony came to get
me. I ran for the park hopin' no one had a heater. we'd
had enough of this white shit. my best friend was jewish.
he was never the same after all of this.

nessun dorma, camp petawawa, 1940

"My head was still resonant with song. . ." – Mario Duliani

they sent hundreds of italian men to petawawa. to sit out
the war just in case they tried to start a revolution. just in
case they turned the whole place upside down.

they sang on the train going up
sang in corners of the camp like shy birds
blew out a village tune at midday
threw together a mandolin band
plucked the corners of their hearts
like lost balding barbers of seville

at night without women no one slept
they hummed a baritone of blues
arias of ancient operas never written down

these spies
these forgotten fascists
of backyard gardens
and homemade wine
sang until *il duce* hanged
sang until the gates swung open
until they felt their wives
sleeping quietly beside them again

mamma corleone

mario and francis got it wrong. vito corleone, the
godfather, didn't run the family. it was his wife. she sat in
shadows. spoke to him with her eyes. sent messages
through food. the amount of salt in pasta sauce. the
configuration of pizza toppings. the strength of his
espresso. all held meaning.

to her he listened. could not refuse the warm touch of
her smile. soft whispering voice in his ear.
they must show you respect. they must fear you.

she knew the weight of his mind from the way he sighed
as his body sank next to hers.
the way his heart beat beneath the palm of her hand. she
told him what to do and he would do it.

tomatoes

alla maniera di George Elliott Clarke

I got passionate *pomodori freschi* big red fat ass sons-of-bitches tomatoes. round firm mother fuckers perfect for salad. I got tiny testicle cherry tomatoes bouncing up a storm like you wouldn't believe. watermelon-sized beefsteak tomatoes ready for a hot veal *sangwich* if you know what I mean. how about some smooth virgin plum *pomodori* to make the best salsa from here to halifax? *caro mio*, you know who started all of this? columbus found *pomodori* for you and me in 1493.

boh

for Luciano

i.

stop an italian mid-step
or in the middle of hand gestures
ask them a question on anything
see what happens when they have no idea
go ahead
I dare you

ii.

this verbal shrug of the shoulders
pushing together of the lips
as in the passing of important flatulence
you know the kind
used only to get rid of your brother
or to end a blind date

the mouth turning down
into a robert de niro
mirror frown
you looking at me?
you looking at me?

boh

iii.

like an existential burp
without the angst
a resolved atheist's acclimation
I don't know
I just don't know

who's that guy at the bar?
who do you think's gonna win the game?

what the hell's the poet talking about?

boh

iv.
romulus turns to his brother remus
why are we drinking milk from a wolf?
aeneas steps off his ship
greek blood still dripping down his right arm
why is this strange land shaped like a boot?
when the whole place was burning down
someone yelled
hey, nero why you playing that thing?
we can't forget juliet
nervous she leans over her balcony
wherefore art thou romeo?

boh

v.
we strive to create the perfect image
within the constraint of this language
hold on to the lost moment
in the forgotten lyrics of some ancient prayer
the sweetness of that syllable
the weight of light in the room
the gesture empty that still escapes us
why?

boh

elvis in the bathroom

I'm reading my elvis poem
to len gasparini, jim christy
and luciano iacobelli

feels like I've just been asked to play
for bird, dizzy and trane
man what a trip

he says, "hey, you wrote an elvis poem
why don't you read it?"
"what, right here in the middle of this party?"
len leans in
his voice as raspy as miles in the eighties
"let's go somewhere
where it's quiet."

it's like luciano's handed me a horn
play it man
burn up the night
like a motherfucker

four of us standing around
between the toilet and the shower
len lights a cigarette
like some secret signal
I step into my poem
jim christy smiles golden
luciano takes in the scene like an art house director

when I'm done it's silent
cigarette smoke swirls out the open door
len says, "you know he died in the bathroom
so this makes sense"

in walks a woman
we turn as if caught in some illicit act
she asks, "what are you guys doing?"

oh, nothing just reading some poetry

for you

after Leonard Cohen

for you
I will be a *mafioso*
wear my suits double-breasted
talk in croaking *sotto voce*
at the back of darkened strip clubs
and make offers
that can only be accepted

for you
I will be an opera *italiano*
sing in deep *crescendos*
wave a white *fatsoletto*
and gain one hundred pounds
eating bowls of *manicotti marinara*

for you
I will be a bricklayer *dago*
whistling at young passing girls
and make *vino* in my garage
after the slaughter of backyard chickens

for you
I will be a world cup wop
and hang flags from my car
honk through rush-hour traffic
and bleed green white and red
until the ref blows his whistle

microphone

"I discovered very early that my instrument wasn't my voice. It was the microphone." – Frank Sinatra

a hairbrush
a clenched fist
before tom cruise in *risky business*
I ran through the empty house in underwear
stereo blasting *men at work*
lips soft against the mic
I had all my stage moves down pat

the shower has great acoustics
blue notes wet as I wailed out
in prince-like crescendos

my car became *la scala*
luciano in the passenger seat
carreras in the back
and domingo in the trunk
'cuz he always tries to up-stage
speeding at midnight on the 401
I almost shatter windshields

dancing with you
the dance floor a crowded tokyo subway
I spread my right hand
make it melt into the small of your back
the lobe of your ear brushing my lips
I whisper like a cuban
the words of our wedding song

we're in italy
the air fits like a tailor made boot from *roma*
we take a train and a ferry to the island of *ponza*
where the sun tickles jagged cliffs

laughs at us through the brays of stubborn white goats
in the morning I pop out of bed dancing
with what little hair I have dishevelled
I sing to you
buongiorno, buongiorno amore

now your pregnant belly becomes a microphone
I sing into the nest of our restless second child
my voice echoing up through your body
out the tips of your fingers
twinkle, twinkle little star

when the moon hits your eye

unprepared a slap. a spit from the back of the room. the
night on you and you thought you were above this. had it
figured out. touched once bitten you thought it never
really existed. only for puppies or the weak kneed with
smoke in their eyes. had it all sorted flying solo into the
sunset no need for duets no desire past this one night.
then it hits you. makes you feel like it's standing still and
you're spinning. nothing in control like you're dancing all
day underwater in old *napoli* that's *amore*.

after nine

one breath

i.
I am writing this while holding my breath because I read
about a palestinian painter who goes out and paints on
big canvases in warzones on one breath till he drops but
I can't remember his name but I can see his face and not
a. . .

ii.
in kyudo
the ancient art of japanese archery
it takes months to learn how to stand
how to breathe
how to draw the bow
it takes a lifetime to learn
how to let the arrow release itself
like a forgotten exhalation

iii.
never let
your opponent see
you breathe
he will attack
when you inhale
because you can't
attack while breathing in
one punch
        one breath

iv.
the whole room held its breath
saving all the air for you
waiting
watching to see what you would do
a fish pulled out flailing

you gulped out crying
sucking up the world
your skin reaching for your mother

v.
I can taste garlic
taste last night's salsa
smell it bounce back off the pillow
the breath of dreams
taste of being lost
in a desert of running
of falling
the taste of death
of open caskets
of wood rotting
steaming up
one last time

vi.
hold the note
your eyes closed
forget about the brass
the room
the thing she told you
before you started
play the heat
the sweat down your back
the lost time
the pressure in your head
the pain in your right ankle
blow till it's all gone

after nine

baby, the kids are asleep
      and the tea is steeping

baby, let me rub
      the day out of your feet
tell you stories about tomorrow

the world is warming on a global scale
      and it only feels safe under this blanket

let me make you laugh
      with imitations of our children
as the clock runs out of time

baby, can you feel the seasons slip into years?
      feel the weight of this basement on your shoulders?

I think the kettle's screaming bloody murder
      and the boys are dreaming of trains again

if I could win a million dollars
      we could never be this rich

kiss me

adagio
lips hardly touching
just the whisper of
the moment anticipated

lento
deep slow breaths
lento moderato
growing from
the back of the throat
moderato espressivo

kiss me
tranquillamente
your tongue starting
its *andante* explorations

kiss me now *allegro*
vivace like you mean it
like the phone's on fire
we're late for work
the kids are waking up in fits

kiss me
prestissimo
before the water
boils over

she is

she's the pause before the start. she's the drum-line. she's
the bass. the clarinet. she's the sighed whisper in the
trumpet. she's the cry. the clearing of his throat before he
fills the church with vows. she's the fall of early snow. the
memory of the crackle of a record. she's the open door.
the violin. she's the slap on skin. she's the moon's spin.
she's the open window. the warm breeze. she's the silence
in the dark when it's all about to close.

roses

soft sub-rosa whispers under petals. in the dry palms of
lovers. held wet between lips of tangoed up dancers. the
growing of thorns when cupid shot an arrow in a rose
garden by mistake. they bleed from hot veins. from the
red of scarlet letters that spell out sin in lost latin. your
lips perfect velvet roses chapped from winter now bloom
into the fullness of spring kisses. time to dead-head
through forgotten afternoons. *roses are red, roses are red,
roses are red. . .* sales were down last year. the florist tells
me of women who call her crying because their roses
haven't opened. she tells them to check the water but
really wants them to check their hearts for unforgiving
truths. remember this as your grip on rose hips tightens.
they contain more vitamin c than fruits and vegetables.
cook red roses into a sweet jam and spread it all around
the lip of a trumpet, like miles did before playing into
the deep cool jazz-filled night. the scent of roses melting
into the air a sweet smoke. come on robbie, *my luve's like
a red, red rose?* it wilts. it dies. it feeds the fungus of a
globally warmed month of june. roses overflowing with
subsexual sighs soak red into thorns wrapped to make a
crown of new found love. place a petal on the tongues of
dead husbands to sweeten the breath of the hereafter. I
can hear her voice before falling asleep a rose is a rose is
a rose. . .

al dente

the perfect moment. not the overcooked soggy feeling in the back of your throat when you don't know what to say like on the first date when I told you that I don't believe in marriage. the perfect light. the sun sitting just right. just so. holding them for the first time. the hospital room spinning. the firmness of that moment. the words forming nicely in your mouth like they were meant to be there. like now. years later when I tell you that you heard me all wrong. I know you don't believe me.

you've had a cold for a month

cooking curry blind
the masala of recipes
written in your blood

culinary improvisation
the bass line of the coconut milk
the spices fill the house
a saxophone of smells

you ask me
stuffed up
your voice cute like a little girl's
can you smell this?

dip my head
down low
into the pot
my brain filling
like a calcutta wedding

the ear of dionysus

I want to take you there
before sunset
before children

leave you at the entrance
your skin in the half-light
looking like a true sicilian

I had my nonna fooled
when I told her
you were from *taormina*

I'd walk in deep
let my voice come to you
in whispers
read to you from guide books

> *legends say the tyrant dionysus of siracusa used the*
> *cave as a prison*
> *the perfect acoustics let him eavesdrop on the plans*
> *and secrets of his captives*
> *some say he carved the cave in its shape to amplify*
> *the screams of prisoners*

I'd be your prisoner
scream *ti amo*
till my ears bled
hug the cave wall
and ask you to marry me
this would be better
than in some toronto restaurant

I'd whisper
the names of our children
let the syllables reach you
in soft caresses down your arm
smooth belly
pulling you at the ankle

I'd be quiet
standing in the hallow dim-light
the sound of my heart
against the cold cave walls
and wait for you to find me

lasso the moon

what is it you want?
I ain't no jimmy stewart but just say the word
by this lake
that nudges up against the night sky
feels like we're all wet behind the ears sometimes
can you see these stars
fresh from the sunset?

you want the moon?
stand back
I'll throw a lasso around it
pull it down
a gift
for you to swallow
and moonbeams'd shoot out of your fingers
toes
the ends of your hair
to light our way home

maybe I'll just kiss you instead
pull you close to me warm
I'll show you
some kissing . . .

daisies

I have dreamt of daisies
turn my hand over
spreading a wet fan of fingers
open to reveal a single orange gerbera
palmed moments before
like some cheap corner store magician
you hire at the last minute

I open my mouth
stick out my tired tongue
the same flower this time red
as a rose as a rose as a rose
makes me sing like billie
on her last album

      daisies at each table
      spindles of happy faces
      on our wedding day
      night a memory of bouquets
      I take off your wedding dress
      falling from you like petals

     she loves me
          loves me not
               she loves me
                    loves me
                         me

hold

hold her. feel the way you fit together. the bones. flesh. the blood pulling hard. hold her. reach up feel her hair. breathe into her neck. hold her. the back of her head into your palm. hold her until you don't know who's hugging who. hold her like a husband who has just found out. like a husband who has just been told. hold her like a husband who can no longer hold the day crumbling between his fingers. like a husband who knows the meaning of prognosis. hold her like a husband who can do nothing. hold her until she lets go.

a dream

wake up in the morning with my shoes on
    with the radio bleeding
        my shoes on
            the day breaks
       with my shoes on
         and all of it
between yesterday and this
          breath
    shoes on
          last night
in your dream you saved my life
    from a serial killer
you never told me if
    he had a knife to my throat
    gun to my chest
    stalked me after dark
 you never told me
    what he smelled like

in your dream you saved my life

but didn't catch him

    maybe tonight
        maybe
          baby
       tonight
with my shoes on

a night in paris

I ask you to translate
the argument
outside our window

I peek through curtains
waiting for a french gunshot

the shared toilet
halfway up the spiral staircase
curved door
you need to sit sideways
just to fit

in the morning
I look for blood
on the curb
as you start
our slow hunt
for baguettes

room

I could just drive
drive and drive
down this driveway
and not stop
ram into the neighbour's guest bedroom
living room
roll down the window
reach for the remote
and change the channel

like the woman in brampton
who mistakes the gas pedal
for the brake
opens a hole in
the wall of my wife's
childhood bedroom
a portal into her memory

I get a long list of everyone who
has ever slept in that room
the chameleon changes of wall colours
the posed fading sepia photographs
of couples in calcutta
uncles in uniform
eyes cut into this millennium
welcoming me into the mix of this family
into spices I have never known

masala of conversation
pulls me back to the party
I put the finishing touches on emil's diaper
anticipating a second car crash
the neighbourhood mistaking this room
for a shortcut

christmas eve

the shape of your shoulders at the sink. the rain melting
postcard snow turns the night into slush. she's in labour
in a barn somewhere in the memory of time. shepherds
can't sleep. stars burn dreams. the breath of stunned cows
and horses heats fear. is he as nervous about something
going wrong as I was? stuffing stockings I can hear santa
squeezing through the chimney in the heads of our boys
between sugarplums, robots and trains. you turn to the
sound of me standing there.

poetics

I could speak directly to the reader. talk about the page.
the syntax. write from the text's point of view or as
though I was a shoe in the closet or the poet who knows
he's writing words as signifiers to the signified. breaking
the fourth wall. the fifth dimension. the missing link. the
link between reader and text and meaning. it's all about
what you bring to the page. it's all about what you're
wearing.

I could stand up and hum till my chest was about to
explode. cup my hands over my face fanning them so I
sound like a clucking chicken in heat beside a red
wheelbarrow glazed with rain water. I could call up three
of my friends and have them scream into a microphone
as I chop on their backs lightly with the edges of my
hands causing their voices to quiver like leaves on trees
in a soft breeze. the audience can only understand a
fragment of what I feel.

I will make my poems mathematical equations. give each
letter a numeric value based on its order in the alphabet.
L=12, O=15, V=22, E=5. 12+15+22+5=64. this is the sum
of all my feelings for you. I will fill our tiny house with
sixty-four roses and sneak into the mid evening backyard
with sixty-four fat guys playing sixty-four blue ukuleles
and sing sixty-four love songs in sixty-four languages. I
will quit my job at sixty-four and stay home and write
you love poems that only contain sixty-four words, sixty-
four vowels, sixty-four syllables. I will type it all using
only my index fingers on an old commodore sixty-four
computer.

all I know is that in the middle of the night, half asleep
in my half of the bed, half moon, half light you reached
across the space between us. your hand fishing for my
arm. you slipped it into and up my short shirt sleeve.
your palm opened and fingers wrapped around my upper
arm like an octopus over a forgotten rock at the ocean's
bottom. you drifted away slowly into sleep. your
rhythmic breathing lulling our second child growing
nameless in the warm pit of your belly.

when I think of you dying I tremble

like a treble clef on a sheet of music for a band in an impromptu outdoor concert caught in summer-rain and you know that gust of wind that comes right before a downpour? it whips up the trombonist's copy of the piece written by the guitarist's girlfriend who's a visa student from seoul. flicks in the air a premature autumn leaf before the rain lets loose.

'round midnight

while listening to Thelonious Monk

in dead winter the walls are black saxophone licks and
piano drips of snow melting over dreams of lasagna
afternoons. the boys move through nightmares of
burning houses. cinderella running with one shoe. he's
left standing tracing the silent line of her body against
the moon. every time I turn a puff of cold air sighs
through the bed like a beat of the bass drum. you reach
out for the shape of me as the furnace swallows up
echoes of summer.

divorce

we will get a divorce. let this love crumble and weed over
like a neglected garden. let side glances and
transgressions go untended. this house will fill with
silence and distances will grow until we become strangers
sharing the same air.

the children will know before we do and they will try to
force us into the same rooms with elaborate
subconscious pleas for love. we will avoid their eyes
because that is where we placed carefully the ingredients
of what it is that drew us together. they will learn the
fragility of the heart. the tenuous bond of this thing
called love. the world around them will become liquid.

we will sell the house and get two houses with two sets
of bedrooms two lives two mini-vans and two area codes.
two times two will equal zero. it's in this separateness we
will hear the silence that has grown on us like skin. we
will feel the coldness in the corners of empty rooms and
re-discover our own reflections in bathroom mirrors.

it will happen slowly on some weekend hand-off or late
night fevered phone call. I will see your skin again or
brush the back of your elbow and smell your hair. the
lobe of your left ear. the children will sense this
reincarnated attraction in our voice. the rewind of re-
growth. they will learn the flexibility of the heart's
muscle. the calisthenics of a relationship gone bad then
born again like a lost christian. they will learn the true
meaning of trust, promise and forever.

It is all of this that I never want to teach them.

apologia

if I say it again will it mean anything? like an
incantation. the hocus-pocus of some transubstantiated
moment in a medieval mass. will it make your heart
beat? if palpitations could raise the dead and remember
dreams of wedding marches. in which language will it
hold the most meaning? once it's said look around the
room for fireworks. to say it with my eyes. the flutter of
eyelids. lashes like fingers waving from a sinking cruise
ship. will there be more power if I walk around you three
times counter-clockwise or rub over your heart with the
oil of virgin olives? after hours. after years and children
laughing from the centres of rooms. I will wrap this
house in rhyming couplets like a mad man. fall with me
into beds of burning flowers. drown in the silence before
we are awake. the shape of your left ear. if it was enough
I would write it in seven tongues ripped from the
mouths of seven poets on fresh sicilian papyrus and
wallpaper the neighbourhood in little cut out hearts. dip
my hands in boiling water to wash your hair in the warm
milk of coconuts. your deep summer skin soaking up the
night moon. if I could play the trumpet I'd play it
syncopated in the basement of that parisian bar sending
whispered slow kisses to hover around your sweet head. a
crown of blue smoke.

Acknowledgements

Thanks to Allan Briesmaster, a true Zen master editor. Thank you to all the jazzy hipsters at Quattro Books for their support and vision. Thanks to Luciano Iaccobelli for keeping the beat and his belief in my work. A special thanks to fellow *jazzista*, Chris D'Iorio, who provided amazing feedback and insight along the way. Thanks to cool Paul Zemokhol, for some early manuscript brainstorming. Thanks to Riadh Matti, my hip-karate brother, for coming out to my readings. To Lise Fournier, Lady Day with a brush, thanks for the paintings. To Rob Ackerman, a real jazzman with a camera, thanks for the photos.

Molte Grazie to my father, Salvatore Capilongo, for showing me how to listen to music and to my mother, Carmela Capilongo, for teaching me to read and write in two languages.

Also many thanks to the people who helped by putting up with my daily rants, ravings, bad jokes, jazzy freestyles and poetic missteps, especially the staff and students in the Thornlea Intensive Program, the true hep cats of the classroom.

A deep thank you to Lynda, my first reader, you put the jazz in everything.